Published by BaoBao Bilingual Books

ISBN 978-1-998317-14-1

Cover design by BaoBao Bilingual Books

First Edition: December, 2023

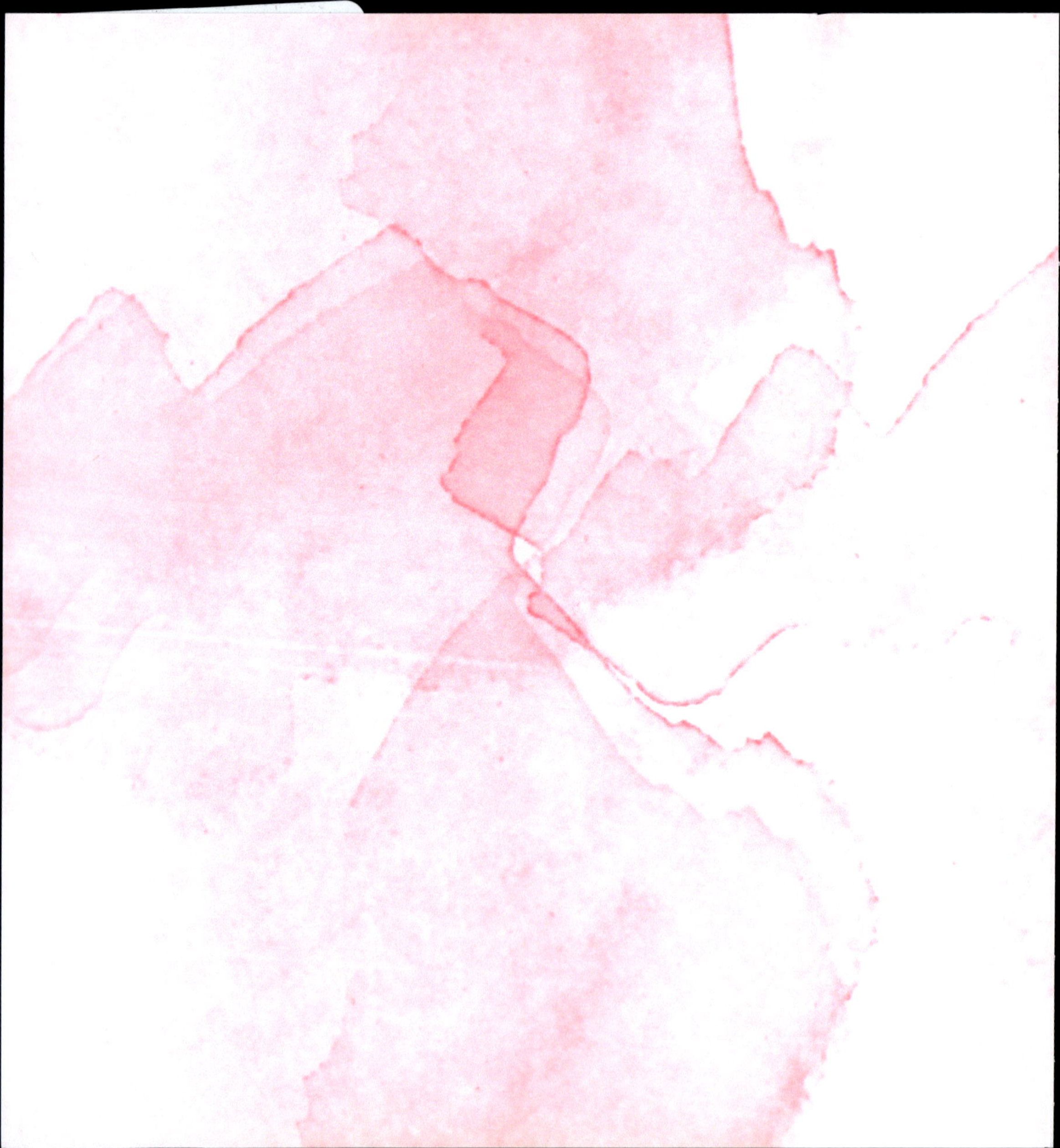

Legend has it that the twelve Chinese Zodiac animals are special guardians who take turns, each year, to watch over the path from the human world to the heavens.

Emperor Jade put in a lot of effort to decide on the twelve Chinese Zodiac animals. With so many animals, who should be chosen?

2

Nine days into the New Year, it was Emperor Jade's birthday. He had a great idea: invite all the animals to celebrate and pick the twelve animals based on when they arrived!

All the animals were super excited and started getting ready.

Some of them
were practicing
jumping around.

Some were learning how to run really fast!

And others were
practicing how to fly high
in the sky!

At that time, the cat and the mouse were very good friends. They received a special message from Emperor Jade and were delighted, so they planned to go together.

The reporting day is almost here, and the cat is a bit worried. Because it loves to sleep in, it's afraid it might miss the reporting time.

The mouse said to the cat, "Don't worry! I'll wake up early and come to get you. We'll go together!"

10

The cat felt really happy
and thanked the mouse
for being its best
friend.

On Emperor Jade's birthday morning, the mouse woke up excited and dashed off cheerfully to attend.

But it got so caught up having fun that it actually forgot to wake up the cat.

13

In the end, the mouse was chosen as one of the twelve Chinese Zodiac animals.

Poor cat! It woke up too late and couldn't report in time, missing the chance to become one of the Zodiac animals.

The cat was really angry and thought it was the mouse's fault.

So, from that time on, whenever the cat saw the mouse, it couldn't resist chasing after it.

The mouse could
only run away as
fast as it could.

But even though the cat was always chasing,
this story never had an end.

They were
always chasing
and running,
and they never
stopped,
forever and
ever.

www.ingramcontent.com/pod-product-compliance
Lightning Source LLC
Chambersburg PA
CBHW042141030726

47599CB00002B/567